Co-Intelligence

The Human Side of Machine Intelligence"

The Unbelievable Story of Human-AI Collaboration and What It Means for Our Future

MUSKAN BEN

TABLE OF CONTENT

INTRODUCTION

A New Era of Collaboration

Artificial intelligence was once the stuff of science fiction, a realm where machines that could think, learn, and collaborate with humans seemed both thrilling and terrifying. Today, that fiction has become reality. AI has stepped into the very fabric of our lives, quietly transforming the way we work, learn, and create. From boardrooms to classrooms, from startups to sprawling corporations, this invisible force is reshaping the future faster than most of us can comprehend. But the most fascinating aspect of this transformation isn't the machines themselves—it's the way humans are adapting to live, work, and grow alongside them.

This book isn't just about artificial intelligence; it's about what happens when human ingenuity meets machine precision. It's about the unexpected partnerships forming in workplaces, the groundbreaking innovations being unleashed in classrooms, and the entirely new ways of thinking that AI has sparked. More importantly, it's about you—whether you realize it or not, you're already living in a world where AI is quietly influencing decisions, shaping careers, and opening doors to possibilities once thought impossible. The question isn't whether AI will affect you; it's how prepared you are to embrace its potential.

Imagine having a co-worker who never sleeps, a mentor who knows every book ever written, or a collaborator who can brainstorm a thousand ideas in the time it takes you to sip your coffee. That's what AI offers. Yet, this book isn't here to paint a utopian picture or sound alarm bells about dystopian futures. Instead, it dives into the gray area where the human side of machine intelligence thrives. This is where creativity, intuition, and empathy intersect with data, algorithms, and neural networks to create something entirely new—something that could redefine what it means to be productive, creative, and innovative.

In the pages that follow, we'll explore the incredible stories of how AI is helping entrepreneurs achieve the impossible, how educators are using it to unlock new ways of learning, and how entire industries are being turned on their heads by this relentless wave of innovation. But we'll also confront the challenges—what does it mean when a machine can outthink a doctor or outperform a seasoned consultant? What happens to jobs, privacy, and even our sense of identity in a world where machines play an increasingly prominent role?

This isn't a book about the technicalities of AI—it's a journey into its human side. You'll discover how ordinary people are harnessing AI to amplify their strengths, break through barriers, and reimagine their futures. You'll see how this technology, while complex and often misunderstood, holds the potential to democratize innovation, making it accessible to anyone willing to learn and adapt.

The story of AI isn't just about machines—it's about the new alliances being formed between human creativity and machine intelligence. It's about the balance between control and collaboration, about embracing uncertainty while daring to explore the unknown. Above all, it's a story about us—about how we rise to the challenge of integrating these tools into our lives and use them to unlock possibilities we never imagined.

So, are you ready to see the world through the lens of co-intelligence? Turn the page, and let's begin a journey that might just change the way you think about your own potential.

CHAPTER 1

The Rise of Artificial Intelligence

Artificial intelligence began as a whisper of possibility, a bold idea imagined by visionaries who dared to think that machines could one day mimic human intelligence. It was in the mid-20th century when pioneers like Alan Turing asked, "Can machines think?" This question marked the birth of AI as a theoretical pursuit, one that would remain confined to academic debates and speculative fiction for decades. Early efforts produced programs that could play chess, solve mathematical problems, and mimic basic reasoning, but these were far from intelligent. They were fragile systems that operated within narrow confines, offering a glimpse of what might one day be possible.

The journey from theoretical speculation to practical application was not a straight path. The 1970s and 1980s saw what came to be known as the "AI winters," periods where funding dried up and optimism waned due to unmet expectations. But in the 1990s, things began to shift. Advances in computing power, combined with the rise of the internet and the availability of massive datasets, gave AI the fuel it needed to grow. Machine learning emerged as a transformative approach, where instead of programming specific instructions, systems could learn patterns from data. Suddenly, AI wasn't just a distant dream—it was becoming a practical tool.

The 21st century marked a turning point. Neural networks, once considered too computationally expensive to be feasible, made a comeback. Researchers discovered that stacking these networks into multiple layers—a concept known as deep learning—could produce remarkable results. This breakthrough led to the development of systems capable of recognizing images, understanding speech, and even translating languages with uncanny accuracy. AI began to find its way into everyday life, powering voice assistants, search engines, and recommendation systems. But as impressive as these achievements were, they were only a prelude to what came next.

The advent of generative AI was nothing short of revolutionary. Unlike earlier systems, which were designed to analyze and respond, generative AI could create. From generating realistic images to crafting coherent and contextually aware text, these systems blurred the line between human creativity and machine capability. The key to this transformation was the rise of large language models—massive AI systems trained on billions of words from books, articles, and conversations. These models, such as OpenAI's GPT-3 and GPT-4, Google's Gemini, and others, demonstrated an astonishing ability to understand and generate language. They didn't just respond to queries; they could write essays, compose poetry, and even simulate human conversations.

What made these advancements truly remarkable wasn't just their technical sophistication—it was their accessibility. AI, once confined to research labs and billion-dollar corporations, began to trickle into the hands of everyday people. Tools built on these large language models made it possible for anyone to leverage AI's power, whether to brainstorm ideas, automate tasks, or enhance creativity. This shift marked AI's evolution from a technical tool to a democratizing force, empowering individuals and small businesses in ways previously unimaginable.

At the heart of this revolution are what experts call "frontier models"—the most advanced AI systems available today. Models like GPT-4 and Gemini have become synonymous with cutting-edge innovation, setting new benchmarks in understanding and generating language. These systems are not only more powerful but also more versatile, capable of performing tasks across domains with minimal human input. Their impact extends far beyond individual use; they are transforming industries, from healthcare to finance, and challenging the very fabric of how work gets done.

As we stand on the precipice of a new era, the rise of AI is more than just a technological milestone. It's a cultural and societal shift, a force that is redefining what's possible for individuals, businesses, and humanity at large. It's not just about what AI can do—it's about how we choose to use it. The story of AI is still being written, but one thing is clear: we are no longer asking whether machines can think. We are now exploring how they can think with us, and what that partnership means for our future.

CHAPTER 2

AI as a Co-Worker

Artificial intelligence is no longer just a tool; it's a collaborator. The age of AI as a co-worker has arrived, and with it comes a fundamental redefinition of how we approach work. Unlike traditional technologies that replaced manual labor, AI has become a complement to human skills, enhancing our capabilities rather than rendering them obsolete. It's not about replacing the worker; it's about redefining the role, creating a dynamic partnership between human intuition and machine precision.

In industries across the board, AI is making its presence felt in profound ways. Take writing, for example. Tasks that once took hours of brainstorming and careful crafting can now be accelerated with AI's help. Need a marketing pitch? AI can generate drafts in seconds, offering multiple angles and ideas that can be refined by human creativity. Writers use AI to overcome creative blocks, refine language, and explore perspectives they might not have considered. The process isn't just faster— it's richer, more dynamic, and collaborative in ways previously unimaginable.

Beyond writing, AI is revolutionizing data analysis and decision-making. Consider the overwhelming volume of data that modern businesses generate daily. Extracting meaningful insights from this sea of information used to require teams of analysts and weeks of effort. Now, AI can sift through mountains of data in minutes, identifying patterns, forecasting trends, and offering actionable insights. In finance, AI systems flag anomalies in transactions that could indicate fraud. In healthcare, they analyze patient records to predict outcomes and recommend treatments. AI doesn't just crunch numbers; it connects dots, helping humans make better decisions faster.

One of the most fascinating ways to think about AI as a co-worker is to liken it to a "first-year PhD intern." Like a fresh graduate with boundless potential, AI is capable of remarkable feats but requires guidance to reach its full capacity. It can draft reports, design prototypes, and even simulate complex scenarios, but it needs human oversight to ensure accuracy and alignment with objectives. This analogy highlights the dynamic interplay between human expertise and AI's computational power. The human sets the vision, provides context, and fine-tunes the results, while AI handles the heavy lifting and generates insights.

The integration of AI into workflows isn't without its challenges. One of the biggest hurdles is trust. Can we trust AI to make decisions that align with human values? While AI excels at processing information, it can also make mistakes—sometimes glaring ones—because it lacks the nuanced understanding of context that humans bring. Ensuring that AI operates transparently and ethically is a critical component of successful collaboration.

Another challenge is resistance to change. For many, the idea of working alongside an AI feels foreign or even threatening. Employees may worry that relying on AI diminishes their value or makes their jobs redundant. Organizations need to address these fears by emphasizing AI's role as an enabler, not a competitor. Training programs that help employees understand how to use AI effectively can transform apprehension into empowerment, showing workers how the technology amplifies their abilities rather than undermines them.

Despite these challenges, the opportunities are immense. AI as a co-worker has the potential to level the playing field, giving small businesses access to capabilities that were once the domain of large corporations. It can democratize innovation, allowing individuals with minimal technical expertise to create, solve, and achieve at unprecedented levels. For large organizations, AI offers a way to optimize operations, improve decision-making, and foster innovation across teams.

The collaboration between humans and AI is reshaping what it means to work. It's not just about efficiency; it's about expanding what's possible. As AI continues to evolve, so too will the nature of our roles, pushing us to focus on creativity, strategy, and the uniquely human traits that machines cannot replicate. In this new era, AI isn't just a co-worker—it's a catalyst for human potential, challenging us to reimagine the future of work and the part we play in it.

CHAPTER 3

The Entrepreneurial Revolution

The entrepreneurial landscape is undergoing a profound transformation, driven by the rise of artificial intelligence. Once considered the domain of highly skilled individuals with access to vast resources, entrepreneurship is now more accessible than ever, thanks to AI's ability to bridge gaps in expertise and amplify human potential. In this new era, AI doesn't just serve as a tool—it becomes a co-founder, stepping into roles that traditionally required entire teams of specialists.

For many entrepreneurs, AI is a silent partner capable of taking on some of the most challenging aspects of starting and scaling a business. Need a fully functional website but don't know how to code? AI can build it. Struggling to create a compelling marketing campaign? AI can generate ad copy, craft social media strategies, and even analyze audience engagement. From designing prototypes to conducting market research, AI fills gaps in skills that might otherwise have held entrepreneurs back. Its speed and efficiency empower founders to focus on vision and strategy while delegating technical, creative, or repetitive tasks to the machine.

Real-world examples illustrate the impact of AI on entrepreneurship. Consider a young founder with a brilliant idea but no technical background. In the past, they might have struggled to bring their concept to life, relying on costly external resources or facing long delays in development. Today, with AI at their disposal, they can generate product designs, simulate user experiences, and even create fully operational prototypes with minimal effort. Entrepreneurs in industries ranging from e-commerce to software development are leveraging AI to scale rapidly, outpacing competitors who rely solely on traditional methods.

The allure of AI lies not just in its capabilities but in the way it levels the playing field. It dismantles the myth that successful entrepreneurship requires innate traits or superhuman abilities. Overconfidence, often touted as a hallmark of entrepreneurs, may drive people to start businesses, but it doesn't guarantee success. Research reveals that disciplined experimentation, strategic decision-making, and effective management are far more critical to long-term outcomes. AI supports these processes, acting as a guide for hypothesis testing, refining business models, and evaluating potential pivots. By integrating AI into their workflows, entrepreneurs can make data-driven decisions that significantly increase their chances of success.

AI also excels in areas where entrepreneurs often struggle. Pitching to investors, for example, requires a combination of clarity, persuasion, and market insight. AI can analyze trends, compile data into compelling narratives, and even simulate pitch sessions to help founders refine their delivery. Scaling a business, another daunting challenge, becomes more manageable with AI's ability to streamline operations, optimize supply chains, and predict market shifts. In many ways, AI transforms entrepreneurship from an unpredictable venture into a more structured, data-informed pursuit.

However, with these opportunities come ethical considerations. The use of AI in entrepreneurship raises questions about transparency, accountability, and fairness. For instance, how do founders ensure that the AI systems they use don't perpetuate biases or create unintended harm? What happens when AI-generated content blurs the line between originality and replication? Entrepreneurs must navigate these challenges with care, setting ethical guidelines for how AI is deployed and ensuring that their ventures align with broader societal values.

The entrepreneurial revolution driven by AI is not just about achieving more—it's about achieving differently. It challenges long-held assumptions about who can be an entrepreneur and what it takes to succeed. By embracing AI as a partner, founders can focus on what they do best: innovating, connecting, and creating. The combination of human ingenuity and machine intelligence is opening doors to possibilities that were once out of reach, marking the dawn of a new era in entrepreneurship.

CHAPTER 4

Education in the Age of AI

Education is undergoing a seismic shift, driven by the transformative power of artificial intelligence. In classrooms that once relied on passive lectures and traditional teaching methods, AI is creating new possibilities for how students engage with knowledge. The age-old model of learning, where teachers deliver information and students passively absorb it, is giving way to a more dynamic, interactive, and personalized approach. AI is not merely a tool for education—it's reshaping the very foundation of how we learn.

At the heart of this transformation is the shift from passive to active learning. AI-powered tools are making it possible for students to engage with material in ways that were previously unimaginable. Instead of simply listening to lectures, students now participate in activities that require them to apply knowledge, solve problems, and think critically. For instance, AI can simulate real-world scenarios, allowing students to test their understanding in a hands-on way. A biology class might include virtual dissections guided by AI, while a history lesson could immerse students in an interactive timeline of events. These experiences make learning not only more engaging but also more effective.

The flipped classroom model is one of the most significant innovations made possible by AI. In this approach, traditional teaching methods are inverted: students learn basic concepts outside the classroom, often through AI tutors, and then spend class time engaging in collaborative and problem-solving activities. AI tutors play a pivotal role in this model, offering personalized instruction tailored to each student's needs. These systems can identify areas where a student is struggling, provide targeted explanations, and even adapt the pace of learning to match their capabilities. The result is a more inclusive and supportive environment where every student has the opportunity to thrive.

Real-world applications of AI in education go beyond theoretical improvements—they are transforming how assignments are designed and completed. Educators are increasingly asking students to "do the impossible" with AI, encouraging them to tackle projects that would have been unattainable without technological assistance. Imagine a student who has never written a line of code being tasked with developing a functional software application, or a non-designer creating a visually stunning presentation. With AI as a collaborator, these once-daunting challenges become achievable, fostering creativity and confidence in students.

Despite its immense potential, the integration of AI into education is not without challenges. One of the most pressing issues is the rise of academic dishonesty. With AI tools capable of generating essays, solving equations, and completing assignments, the temptation to misuse them is significant. This has led educators to rethink traditional assessment methods, moving toward in-class evaluations and hands-on demonstrations that minimize opportunities for cheating. Schools are also exploring ways to incorporate AI ethically, teaching students to use these tools responsibly while emphasizing the importance of critical thinking and originality.

Adapting to AI-enhanced learning also requires a shift in norms and expectations. Educators must redefine their roles, moving from being sole sources of knowledge to facilitators of learning. This involves not only embracing new technologies but also fostering a culture of curiosity and adaptability in the classroom. Students, too, must learn to navigate the balance between relying on AI for assistance and developing their own skills and insights. The goal is not to replace traditional learning but to augment it, creating a richer, more multifaceted educational experience.

As AI continues to evolve, its impact on education will only deepen. The tools we see today are just the beginning of a revolution that has the potential to make learning more accessible, engaging, and effective for all. By embracing these changes, educators and students alike can unlock new possibilities, preparing for a future where knowledge is not just acquired but actively created in collaboration with technology. In the age of AI, education is no longer confined to the walls of a classroom—it is an ever-expanding frontier of opportunity.

CHAPTER 5

AI as a Coach and Tutor

Artificial intelligence is emerging as one of the most effective tools for personal growth and development, redefining how we learn, improve, and refine our skills. As a coach and tutor, AI has the unique ability to provide personalized guidance, bridging gaps in knowledge and performance that traditional methods often overlook. In this new role, AI offers not just support, but a level of precision and adaptability that feels remarkably human while scaling to meet individual needs in ways human tutors never could.

One of the most promising aspects of AI is its potential as a one-on-one tutor. Unlike traditional classroom settings where students must share attention with peers, AI provides undivided focus, tailoring its teaching to the learner's pace, style, and weaknesses. A student struggling with algebra can receive step-by-step guidance tailored to their understanding, while another mastering advanced calculus can delve deeper into complex problems without delay. This level of customization allows learners to overcome barriers at their own speed, creating a more inclusive and empowering educational experience.

The impact of personalized tutoring is well-documented, most notably in Bloom's "2 Sigma" study, which found that one-on-one tutoring improves student performance by two standard deviations—moving a student from the 50th percentile to the 98th. AI replicates this effect by delivering individualized instruction that mimics the attention and adaptability of a human tutor. Whether it's breaking down a difficult concept, providing instant feedback, or offering encouragement, AI tutors are making the benefits of one-on-one learning accessible to anyone with an internet connection.

AI's role as a coach goes beyond academics. It is increasingly being used to enhance self-improvement and decision-making in both personal and professional contexts. One powerful example is the concept of premortems, where individuals or teams imagine potential failures before starting a project. AI can guide users through this process by prompting them to identify risks, evaluate possible solutions, and prepare for challenges. By fostering this proactive mindset, AI helps users avoid pitfalls and improve the likelihood of success.

Personal performance analysis is another area where AI shines as a coach. By processing vast amounts of data, AI can provide insights into patterns, behaviors, and areas for improvement that might otherwise go unnoticed. Whether it's analyzing a presentation for tone and clarity or evaluating productivity trends over time, AI offers actionable feedback that enables users to refine their skills and achieve their goals. This constant loop of reflection and adjustment creates a pathway to meaningful growth.

For those looking to use AI as a personal tutor or coach, a few practical tips can enhance the experience. First, clarity is key: the more specific you are in your requests, the more targeted and useful the AI's responses will be. For example, instead of asking, "Help me learn biology," specify, "Explain the process of photosynthesis in simple terms." Second, treat the AI as an interactive partner, asking follow-up questions and challenging its suggestions to deepen your understanding. Third, leverage AI's adaptability by experimenting with different prompts and approaches until you find what works best for your learning style.

AI also excels at contextualizing information. A busy professional can request summaries of industry reports written for their specific expertise, while a high school student can ask for explanations tailored to their grade level. By framing its output around the user's context, AI becomes an even more effective guide.

The beauty of AI as a coach and tutor lies in its ability to complement human potential. It doesn't replace the need for curiosity, critical thinking, or creativity; rather, it amplifies these qualities by removing barriers and providing tools to succeed. In this partnership, humans remain at the center, directing the journey while AI provides the map, compass, and extra push to reach new heights. With every interaction, AI reminds us that learning and growth are no longer bound by limits—they are powered by a limitless resource that is as ready to teach as we are to learn.

CHAPTER 6

Redefining the Workplace

Artificial intelligence is fundamentally reshaping the modern workplace, challenging traditional norms, and offering new possibilities for how businesses operate. As AI becomes an integral part of professional settings, it is leveling the playing field, allowing smaller organizations and individuals to compete in ways that were once reserved for well-funded corporations. This shift is not just about technology—it's about transforming workflows, redefining roles, and adapting to a future where AI is a central force in every industry.

One of AI's most profound impacts is its ability to democratize access to advanced tools and capabilities. Tasks that once required entire teams or significant resources can now be accomplished with the help of AI. For example, a small business owner with no formal design training can use AI to create professional marketing campaigns, while a startup can leverage AI-powered analytics to make data-driven decisions previously accessible only to large corporations. By removing barriers, AI empowers professionals to focus on innovation and strategy rather than getting bogged down in technical or repetitive tasks.

Central to this transformation are AI-powered co-pilots and tools designed to assist workers across various domains. In creative industries, co-pilots help generate content, refine ideas, and accelerate production timelines. In finance, they analyze trends, optimize budgets, and flag anomalies. In healthcare, they assist in diagnosing conditions and recommending treatments. These tools don't just enhance productivity; they also enable professionals to focus on the tasks that require uniquely human skills, such as problem-solving, empathy, and critical thinking.

However, the integration of AI into the workplace isn't without challenges. One of the most pressing issues is shadow IT, where employees adopt AI tools without organizational oversight. While this often leads to creative and efficient solutions, it also poses significant risks, such as data breaches, compliance violations, and inconsistent practices. Organizations must strike a delicate balance between encouraging experimentation and maintaining control. Establishing clear policies and guidelines for AI use is essential to harness its benefits while mitigating risks.

Another challenge lies in training employees to use AI effectively. Many professionals, particularly those in traditional industries, may feel overwhelmed or even threatened by the rapid adoption of AI. Addressing this requires a cultural shift, where organizations invest in training programs that not only teach technical skills but also emphasize AI's role as an enabler rather than a competitor. When employees understand how AI can amplify their strengths and make their work more meaningful, resistance often gives way to enthusiasm.

As AI continues to evolve, so too does the nature of jobs and the skills required to perform them. Routine and repetitive tasks are increasingly being automated, pushing workers to adapt and focus on areas where human ingenuity is irreplaceable. For some, this shift will mean learning new skills or transitioning to entirely different roles. For others, it will involve redefining their existing roles to integrate AI seamlessly. The future of work will prioritize adaptability, creativity, and a willingness to embrace lifelong learning as core competencies.

While the transition to an AI-driven workplace presents challenges, it also offers unprecedented opportunities for growth and innovation. Organizations that embrace these changes will find themselves better equipped to thrive in an increasingly competitive landscape. By fostering a culture of collaboration between humans and machines, businesses can unlock new levels of efficiency, creativity, and resilience.

The redefinition of the workplace isn't just about adapting to technology—it's about reimagining what work can be. AI isn't here to replace workers; it's here to elevate them, enabling professionals to do more, achieve more, and focus on what truly matters. In this evolving dynamic, humans and AI are no longer separate entities but collaborators in a shared mission to shape the future of work.

CHAPTER 7

The Human in the Loop

The concept of "the human in the loop" represents a critical balance in the evolving relationship between artificial intelligence and human intelligence. While AI has proven itself to be a transformative tool, capable of extraordinary feats, it is not infallible. Human oversight remains essential to ensure that AI applications are effective, ethical, and aligned with our broader goals. This dynamic partnership between humans and machines highlights the unique strengths each brings to the table and underscores the importance of keeping people at the center of AI-driven processes.

Human oversight in AI applications acts as a safeguard against errors and unintended consequences. AI systems, no matter how advanced, lack the contextual understanding, empathy, and nuanced judgment that humans possess. For instance, an AI tasked with automating a hiring process might inadvertently perpetuate biases present in its training data. A human in the loop can identify and address these biases, ensuring that decisions are fair and inclusive. Similarly, in medical diagnostics, while AI can analyze vast amounts of data to identify potential conditions, a doctor's interpretation remains vital to consider the patient's unique circumstances and history.

The power of human-AI collaboration lies in leveraging their respective strengths. Humans excel at creativity, strategic thinking, and empathy—qualities that machines cannot replicate. On the other hand, AI thrives in areas that demand speed, precision, and the ability to process massive datasets. By delegating repetitive or computationally intensive tasks to AI, humans can focus on higher-order responsibilities that require judgment, innovation, and interpersonal skills. This not only enhances efficiency but also creates opportunities for individuals to contribute in more meaningful ways.

Real-world examples illustrate the impact of successful human-AI collaboration. In journalism, AI tools can quickly analyze large volumes of data, identifying trends or anomalies that reporters can then investigate further. This partnership allows journalists to focus on crafting compelling narratives and asking critical questions. In customer service, AI-powered chatbots handle routine inquiries, freeing human agents to address more complex or emotionally charged issues. In fields like architecture, AI can generate multiple design concepts based on specified parameters, while architects refine and adapt these concepts to meet aesthetic and functional goals.

The role of the human in the loop extends beyond practical applications to encompass ethical considerations. As AI becomes more integrated into our lives, it raises questions about accountability and decision-making. Who is responsible if an AI system makes a harmful or incorrect decision? How do we ensure that AI aligns with human values and societal norms? Keeping humans involved in the process provides a layer of accountability and allows us to guide AI's development and deployment in ways that prioritize fairness, safety, and inclusivity.

Practically, being the human in the loop requires active engagement and critical thinking. It's not enough to simply monitor AI outputs; humans must question, validate, and refine these results to ensure they meet the desired objectives. This means cultivating a culture of collaboration, where humans and AI are seen as partners rather than competitors. It also means equipping individuals with the skills and knowledge to work effectively with AI, from understanding its limitations to optimizing its capabilities.

As AI continues to evolve, the need for human oversight will remain paramount. Machines can do incredible things, but they cannot replicate the values, ethics, and intuition that define humanity. The role of humans in the loop is not to control AI but to guide it, ensuring that it serves as a force for good and aligns with the complexities of the human experience. In this partnership, humans are not diminished by AI's capabilities—they are elevated, empowered to focus on what truly matters while trusting their machine collaborators to handle the rest. Together, this symbiotic relationship has the potential to shape a future that is both innovative and profoundly human.

CHAPTER 8

The Democratization of Innovation

Artificial intelligence is breaking down barriers that once separated technical expertise from creative ambition. By democratizing innovation, AI has made it possible for individuals with little to no technical background to achieve feats that were once the exclusive domain of highly skilled professionals. This transformation is not only empowering individuals but also reshaping industries and economies on a global scale.

At the heart of this democratization is AI's ability to simplify complex tasks. Non-technical users can now build software applications, design marketing campaigns, or analyze vast datasets with tools powered by advanced AI models. For instance, a small business owner who has never written a line of code can use AI to automate customer service workflows, create engaging advertisements, and even optimize pricing strategies. Similarly, educators can use AI to develop personalized lesson plans, and artists can generate intricate designs with just a few prompts. By removing technical barriers, AI opens doors for creativity and innovation, allowing more people to participate in problem-solving and creation.

The implications of this shift extend far beyond individuals. Industries are witnessing unprecedented transformations as AI accelerates processes, improves outcomes, and reduces costs. In healthcare, for example, AI has demonstrated an ability to outperform doctors in specific tasks, such as diagnosing certain diseases from medical images. By analyzing vast amounts of data with precision and consistency, AI can detect patterns that might elude even the most experienced practitioners. This doesn't mean AI replaces doctors; rather, it augments their capabilities, allowing them to focus on patient care while relying on AI for diagnostic support.

In finance, frontier AI models are surpassing specialized tools that once dominated the industry. AI can analyze market trends, predict financial risks, and optimize investment portfolios with remarkable accuracy. For example, large language models like GPT-4 have been shown to outperform domain-specific models in tasks like stock predictions. This is because their extensive training enables them to draw insights from a broader range of data, providing a level of versatility that traditional tools lack. As a result, financial institutions are increasingly adopting AI to gain a competitive edge and navigate the complexities of global markets.

The democratization of innovation has also given rise to countless success stories, showcasing how AI is transforming the lives of early adopters. Consider the entrepreneur who, with no prior experience, used AI to develop a functional app and secure funding within days. Or the nonprofit organization that leveraged AI to optimize donation campaigns, reaching more donors and raising funds more efficiently than ever before. These examples highlight the potential of AI to unlock opportunities for anyone willing to embrace its capabilities.

However, the benefits of AI democratization come with challenges. As access to these powerful tools becomes more widespread, there is a risk of misuse, whether intentional or unintentional. Ensuring that AI is used responsibly requires education, regulation, and a commitment to ethical practices. Organizations and individuals must prioritize transparency and accountability, fostering a culture of trust as AI becomes an integral part of innovation.

The broader economic impact of this transformation is profound. By enabling more people to innovate and contribute, AI is driving productivity gains and economic growth. Small businesses and startups, empowered by AI, can now compete with larger, more established players, fostering a more dynamic and competitive marketplace.

In turn, industries are becoming more efficient, resilient, and adaptive to change.

The democratization of innovation is redefining the boundaries of what's possible. AI is not just a tool for the elite or the highly skilled—it is a force that empowers everyone to participate in shaping the future. By embracing this new reality, individuals and organizations can harness AI's potential to solve problems, create value, and drive progress. The age of innovation is no longer confined to a select few; it is an open invitation for anyone to explore, experiment, and achieve.

CHAPTER 9

Risks and Challenges

As artificial intelligence continues to transform the world, its rise comes with significant risks and challenges that cannot be ignored. While AI's potential to enhance lives and industries is extraordinary, its widespread adoption raises pressing ethical concerns, long-term uncertainties, and the potential for societal disruption. Navigating these challenges requires a balanced approach that safeguards humanity while fostering innovation.

One of the most immediate ethical concerns surrounding AI is its capacity to generate misinformation. AI-powered systems, capable of creating text, images, and videos that mimic reality, have blurred the line between fact and fabrication. Deepfake technology, for example, can produce videos indistinguishable from genuine footage, posing threats to political stability, personal privacy, and trust in media. Beyond misinformation, AI's inherent biases—rooted in the data it is trained on—can perpetuate or even exacerbate existing inequalities. Left unchecked, biased algorithms risk reinforcing systemic discrimination, particularly in areas like hiring, policing, and lending.

Long-term uncertainties further complicate the picture. As researchers push toward the development of artificial general intelligence (AGI)—machines capable of performing any intellectual task a human can—debates intensify about the implications of such advancements. Will AGI surpass human intelligence, and if so, what safeguards are necessary to ensure it remains aligned with human values? Proponents see AGI as the ultimate tool for solving humanity's greatest challenges, from climate change to disease eradication. Skeptics, however, warn of existential risks, fearing that an AGI operating without proper controls could act in ways harmful to society. These questions remain unanswered, adding layers of complexity to AI's trajectory.

The rapid integration of AI into the workplace also raises concerns about job displacement and societal disruption. Automation has already begun to replace roles in manufacturing, logistics, and customer service, and AI's expanding capabilities threaten to encroach on white-collar professions as well. While AI is expected to create new jobs, the transition could leave many workers unprepared, leading to widespread economic instability and inequality. Preparing for this shift requires proactive measures, such as retraining programs and investments in education, to ensure that workers can adapt to the demands of an AI-driven economy.

Regulation and policy play a crucial role in addressing these challenges. Striking the right balance between innovation and safeguards is no easy task. Overregulation risks stifling progress, while insufficient oversight could lead to harmful consequences. Policymakers must consider issues such as data privacy, accountability, and transparency when developing frameworks for AI governance. For example, requiring organizations to disclose how their AI systems make decisions can build trust and reduce the risk of misuse. Similarly, establishing standards for data quality and fairness can help mitigate biases in AI algorithms.

Encouraging responsible AI use in industries is another critical aspect of regulation. Companies must be held accountable for the ethical implications of their AI deployments. This includes ensuring that AI systems operate transparently, prioritizing user safety, and avoiding unintended consequences. Industry leaders must also commit to fostering a culture of ethical AI development, investing in tools and practices that align with societal values. Collaboration between governments, businesses, and academic institutions will be essential to establish norms and best practices for responsible AI use.

Despite the challenges, these risks are not insurmountable. By addressing them proactively, we can guide AI's development in ways that maximize its benefits while minimizing its harms. The key lies in acknowledging AI's dual nature: as a powerful force for good and a potential source of disruption. With thoughtful regulation, ethical accountability, and a commitment to education and adaptation, humanity can navigate these risks and harness AI's transformative potential for a better future. The path forward is not without obstacles, but it is one worth pursuing—because the stakes are nothing less than the future of society itself.

CHAPTER 10

The Future of Co-Intelligence

The future of co-intelligence is a vision of humanity and artificial intelligence working in seamless partnership, redefining what is possible in nearly every facet of life. As AI continues to evolve, its capabilities will expand in ways that challenge our understanding of creativity, productivity, and problem-solving. Yet, amid this wave of innovation, one thing remains clear: the role of humans will not diminish but transform, shifting toward tasks that require our uniquely human strengths.

Advancements in AI capabilities are progressing at an unprecedented pace. Systems are becoming more powerful, adaptive, and versatile, handling increasingly complex tasks with precision and efficiency. AI will move from being a tool for assistance to an indispensable collaborator, capable of providing insights, making recommendations, and even initiating solutions autonomously. The promise of frontier models today hints at a future where AI systems understand not only data but also context, culture, and nuance—traits once thought exclusive to human intelligence. This progression will open doors to breakthroughs in medicine, environmental sustainability, education, and countless other fields, accelerating the pace of global progress.

As AI grows more capable, the role of humans in an AI-driven world will evolve. Rather than competing with machines, humans will focus on areas where they excel: creativity, strategy, and innovation. AI will take on repetitive, time-consuming tasks, freeing individuals to explore ideas, develop new strategies, and pursue groundbreaking innovations. In this future, collaboration becomes the key to success. Humans will direct the vision, define the problems, and set the ethical framework, while AI executes, analyzes, and refines with unparalleled speed and precision.

The promise of a "co-intelligent" future is one of synergy rather than substitution. Imagine architects who can instantly generate and refine designs with AI assistance, allowing them to focus on the artistic and functional aspects of their work. Picture scientists using AI to model complex scenarios, enabling them to dedicate more time to experimental creativity. Consider entrepreneurs leveraging AI to manage logistics and operations, leaving them free to concentrate on their vision and growth strategies. In each case, AI acts not as a replacement but as an amplifier of human potential, enabling individuals to achieve more than they ever could alone.

This future is not without its challenges, but it offers an unparalleled opportunity to reshape how we work, create, and solve problems. Embracing co-intelligence requires a mindset shift—one that values adaptability, continuous learning, and ethical responsibility. Organizations and individuals alike must be willing to experiment with AI, learn from its limitations, and refine its applications. The tools we use today are only the beginning; the real potential lies in how we choose to integrate these capabilities into our lives and societies.

Adapting to this new reality means viewing AI not as a threat but as a partner. By fostering trust, understanding, and collaboration, we can unlock the full potential of co-intelligence, creating a world where innovation is not limited by resources or expertise but fueled by the combined power of human ingenuity and machine precision. This partnership offers a future where challenges that once seemed insurmountable become opportunities, where progress is not a linear march but an exponential leap forward.

The journey toward a co-intelligent future is both exciting and uncertain, but it is one we must embrace. AI's role in our lives will only grow, and the choices we make now will shape how this technology influences generations to come. By focusing on what makes us uniquely human and working alongside AI to amplify those qualities, we can build a future that is not just advanced but also profoundly human. Co-intelligence is not just about machines learning to think—it's about humans learning to think differently, empowered by the possibilities AI brings. Together, this collaboration has the power to redefine what it means to imagine, create, and achieve. The future is not just AI-driven; it is co-intelligent, and it is ours to shape.

CONCLUSION

Embracing the Human Side

Artificial intelligence is not here to replace us—it is here to amplify what we, as humans, are capable of achieving. This is the essence of co-intelligence: a partnership where human creativity, intuition, and ethics converge with machine precision, speed, and analytical power. Through this book, we have explored the many dimensions of this collaboration, from its transformative impact on education and entrepreneurship to its role in reshaping industries, redefining work, and addressing global challenges.

AI has shown us how it can level the playing field, empowering individuals without technical expertise to achieve extraordinary things. It has become a co-worker, a coach, a tutor, and even a collaborator, making once-impossible tasks attainable. From the classroom to the boardroom, AI is driving a profound shift in how we think, learn, and innovate. At the same time, we've acknowledged the risks and challenges that come with this rapid advancement—issues of bias, misinformation, ethical responsibility, and societal disruption that demand thoughtful solutions.

Throughout these chapters, one truth remains constant: AI is not a standalone entity; it is a tool, a partner that relies on human oversight, guidance, and purpose. It is in the hands of people—entrepreneurs, educators, leaders, and innovators—that AI's true potential is realized. This collaboration is not about surrendering control to machines but about leveraging their capabilities to elevate our own.

The future of co-intelligence holds boundless possibilities, but it requires action. It calls on us to adapt, to embrace lifelong learning, and to foster a culture that values both human ingenuity and technological progress. This is not a time for hesitation or resistance—it is a time for curiosity, experimentation, and courage. By integrating AI thoughtfully and responsibly, we can create a future where technology serves as a force for good, driving innovation while preserving the values that define us as human beings.

This is your invitation to step into that future. Whether you are an entrepreneur exploring new ventures, a professional rethinking your role, or an individual seeking to understand the world around you, the possibilities of co-intelligence are within your reach. Embrace the human side of this partnership, and you will find that AI is not a threat to your potential—it is an enabler of it.

Together, we have the opportunity to shape a future that is not just advanced but also deeply human. By embracing co-intelligence, we can build a world where innovation is inclusive, progress is equitable, and every challenge is met with the combined strength of human creativity and machine intelligence. This is the promise of co-intelligence—a future we can create, together.